If You Build It, LIFE Will Come

*How to Build Your Dream Product Idea
and Engineer the World into Your Playground*

By Margot Sandy

Table of Contents

Chapter 1

Toys, Chub Years and a Large Collection of Ninja Turtles

The year was 1994, the scene was Harris Hill Elementary School in Penfield, NY where a girl in the midst of her "chub years" was selling cupcakes out of her locker to get more money for extra chips that day. That girl was me, Margot (aka the person on the back of this book / the author...stay with me people). Little did I know that this ploy for more delicious carbs was the start of my entrepreneurial journey. I had developed a routine of grabbing extra desserts before leaving the house to refill the inventory in my 3rd grade locker. Consequently, this was only the first year of a four-year phase to be largely defined not by my savvy business skills, but by the extra baggage residing around my midsection. Some might have said it was baby weight, but when you can walk, talk and dispense baked goods out of your school locker, you've passed that crucial baby fat stage. I was short and stout with a face dominated by large colorful glasses, a signature look of feathery bangs, a clear plastic visor, a neatly tucked pink or purple turtleneck or a novelty t-shirt, and zipperless jeans that my mom purchased in the boys husky section at Walmart to fit my frame. I was the female version of Steve Urkel.

This incredibly awkward stage coincided with realizing what I wanted to do when I grew up. And Tom Hanks actually played a role in this life-path decision. Not sure how I got my hands on his movie Big, which was a box office hit 6 years prior. I was instantly struck by the film about a boy that plays a fortune teller machine and wishes that he's "big" or grown up. His wish soon comes true and he ends up working at a toy company. The details are sketchy on how he lands this coveted position, but working at a toy company quickly became my dream. I had no idea how I was going to achieve this, I just knew (in my single digit years) that I wanted to play with toys for a living.

I was good at math and science and had a love of everything involving blocks. Whether it was Legos, Erector Sets, K'nex or Lincoln Logs, my heart belonged to building things. There were no Barbies in my play world. Of course, I had other toys, a few oddities like a collection of rubber snakes that I would occasionally leave around the house to scare my grandmother when she visited, a stuffed iguana, and an incredibly large teddy bear named Spanky. Though each toy had a fond memory attached to it, they were all side characters in my block-building world. With each passing year, my love of toys grew and began expanding beyond blocks to eccentric gadgets. I remember asking for that one special gift at Christmas time and reflecting back, it tended to be a random piece of electronic equipment, perhaps a toy cash register, a polaroid camera, a mini recording device, even a Palm Pilot. Now when you think about it, why would a middle schooler need a Palm Pilot? There are no urgent meetings to schedule at age 12, no emails to check, no meeting minutes to dictate, but for some reason these gadgets spoke to me and I wanted to play with them and sometimes take them part.

With my dreams of working at a toy company fully taking off, I realized I needed some sort of professional title for myself. The professions Architect and Engineer entered my vocabulary without fully understanding what they meant. I knew my Uncle was an Engineer and I knew an Architect readily used a pencil and ruler (which I was fond of), but other than that I knew nothing of what it meant to have either of those jobs. The only thing I knew was that if I combined my love for toys with one of these

professions, my future was set. Thus emerged my life-

pursuant goal--to become a toy engineer.

Chapter 2

The Michigan Move & Halloween Costumes

As I finished up my "chub years" and entered the "tween" period of my life, my toy dreams were put on hold for a bit. A new love had entered my life--puzzles.

Puzzles are actually a great way to exercise the brain. It gave me an early start to problem solving and combined my love of building things. It was the next level toy. I equate it to a toy graduation of sorts. I was moving up. These were not your average puzzles. They were 3D puzzles and I was addicted to them. These were 500 to 3000 piece masterpieces that you could build into skyscrapers--everything from the Capitol Building to the Eiffel Tower to the Taj Majal to New York City. Each puzzle became a new challenge or obsession to see how fast I could put it together. My completion time for a

1000-piece work was typically less than a week. Little did I know that this period of puzzle building was my first introduction to design and structural engineering.

As I approached that wonderful time in everyone's life known as high school, my family made the decision to move from upstate New York--home of the Syracuse Orangemen, the famed grocery store Wegmans, and a close neighbor of Canada--to lovely Michigan. New York had been my dear home for 13 years and I loved it so. Of course it was a challenge to move and the transition to the Midwest was a little shaky. However, it probably was one of the best things for me, because it taught me to adjust to change, learn how to make new friends and adapt to a new environment. Although this was a move I fought through teenage tantrums, cold shoulders and pure disdain at times, it ultimately had a positive impact on me for the reasons stated, but more importantly, it enabled me to fine tune my craft of building Halloween costumes.

As insane as it sounds, building Halloween costumes (elaborate costumes at that) gave me a strong foundation for my engineering product development path. My costumes, which included everything from Jenga, Ms. Peanut, a Xylophone, and a Parrot in a Cage, became the fun challenge that I looked forward to making each year. It replaced my puzzle fascination. First, I had to learn how to work with different materials. Granted I was using foam board, duct tape and other random supplies, but each costume was a good lesson. It also taught me about attachment methods and what materials bonded best together. This concept of materials was best learned as I put together my SpongeBob Squarepants costume. I wracked my brain trying to figure out how to attach cereal bowl eyes to a spray painted old mattress pad. It really made me think about the structure of the design.

Another skill sharpening moment was when I had to think about meeting the needs of the consumer, which in this case was me. This was best illustrated when I built a giant Dentyne Ice Package costume and could barely walk in it. I had made the mistake of having the costume extend past my knees. Fitting through a door was nearly an insurmountable challenge and when I got stuck in a bathroom stall at the High School Halloween Dance that year, I knew I had to make adjustments to my build techniques. All of this trial and error building helped fine tune some of the very same engineering skills I use today. Hobbies, side projects, and pastimes may not seem to mean a lot at the time, but they are acquired skills and no matter how ridiculous they are (even if they do include face paint and suspenders) they are transferrable in the job

market.

Chapter 3

Sasquash Buddies ... Finding my Crew

Now I know what you're thinking, how could it be tough for a girl like me to make friends at a new school? With my affinity for the Teenage Mutant Ninja Turtles, my Coke bottle glasses, and Halloween costume engineering skills, prospective friends should have been lining up. I know, I don't get it either, but the move to Michigan tested my socialization skills. How do you make connections when you don't know anybody?

There's the classic lunch room scene of walking in when you're the new kid and trying to figure out where to sit. Fortunately for me though, that didn't happen. I actually approached my group prior to the lunchroom face-off, and finding my crew before awkwardness ensues has been my goal ever since.

Taking a look back, little did I know that a U.S. Supreme Court case that had been going on for nine years to switch girl's basketball to the winter (like the boys) instead of the fall in Michigan actually worked in my favor. I played basketball growing up and would play it all throughout school. I started playing basketball at the age of 10 when my Dad put up a hoop for himself in the driveway. I must have known that this sport could lead to much more than the added benefit of shedding a few pounds, so when I moved to Michigan and girl's basketball was playing in the fall at the start of the school year, I was able to meet new people right away that shared a common interest.

I was a shy kid and typically wouldn't jump into my corny jokes at the start of a greeting. However, that first day I was on the basketball court, a girl came up to me, in spite of my friend-repelling feathered bangs, and said "hello". This turned out to be my good friend, Brigitte. It was that single act of kindness that I will always hold so dear.

All you need in life is one good friend...one good friend that you can mooch off of for their friends. (Anyone laughing…no?). In all seriousness, meeting my friend that day made high school a much more bearable experience for me. It's better to share something with someone than to go at it alone. Along with Brigitte, I met four other good friends that will be referenced from here on out as the Sasquash Buddies (not to be confused with Sasquatch, the simian folklore creature). As weird as the name sounds, Brigitte and I co-founded the Sasquash Buddies Club, better known as the SCA (Sasquash Club of America). This would be my first official enterprise. We both had titles, business cards and even a theme song. I imagine if either of us had been legal savvy at the time, we may have acquired an LLC. The name was chosen for reasons I can't remember now and we were the sole members for quite a period of time (go figure!), but that tribe soon thrived.

As the club grew, it only seemed appropriate to produce a newsletter known as *The Sasquash Times*. It was typically a weekly 2-page full color publication that my co-sasquash buddy, Alicia, and I would write. The subscriber list began at about 5, and when you consider the content which was largely comprised of off color jokes, hard hitting stories about the Proboscis monkey (if you've never seen the monkey, please Google now), and inside tales of ribaldry that only the students at Grand Blanc High School would understand, it may come as no shock that number dwindled to about 2 or 3 (myself and Alicia included). However, this really propelled my desire to create and share something (hopefully) enjoyable for others. I am happiest when I am creating or sharing and surrounded by a tribe of some sort. With each new life circumstance, whether I'm making a major move or traveling to a far off country, I take the Michigan experience and look to replicate it in some form or another to try and find that group before the lunch room. The only difference is this time I search for it wearing contact lenses. :)

Chapter 4

College Basketball ...."Get on the Line" and What it Taught Me

High school soon passed and I started my college career at Rochester Institute of Technology (RIT) in Rochester, NY. I had returned to where I had moved from five years prior. RIT is a private university and this nearly 200 year old school is very much known for its academics. Although the college's hockey and a few other sports have done quite well, at the time the women's basketball team was not amongst the athletic elites. To compete in collegiate athletics at this school while pursuing my academic studies was quite the challenge, but I loved the sport. For whatever reason, I've always thrived off of high stress situations and this 4-year experience as a student-athlete was no different.

I'm not sure what drew me most to the sport of basketball, but part of it was you could most often see results from your hard work. There was a direct correlation to putting more practice time in at the gym and track and seeing the results pay off on the court the next season. This was something I thrived on and would notoriously spend my summers focused on the different areas of improvement to get ready for the next season. Pursuing the sport was also good insight into the characters of those around you. You learn a lot about people when they're physically drained. I'm talking about when your body has nothing left after an intense workout or a large amount of running and you and your teammates have to make the decision to keep going or not. This is sheer will. This is grit. Some people don't have it and a sport like basketball brings it out and shines a light on how much fight you really have.

The sport will also instantly tell you who is selfish and hogs the ball for her own accolades or who celebrates more for a shot <u>she</u> made than a shot a teammate makes. And team is what it's all about. The bonus of being part of a team and learning to work with people from all different backgrounds and ages is that it prepares you for teams you may encounter in the real world. Whether you're playing sports or working in an office, you'll encounter people from all walks of life and you have to somehow learn to work together as a cohesive unit. I loved being part of a team and especially in the basketball world you had the added benefit of road trips / away tournaments which gave me the perfect opportunity to test out my latest batch of corny jokes. Finally, there was all that life learning stuff with wins and losses.

Michigan had prepared me well for the next level of basketball. Through the AAU (Amateur Athletic Union) games, summer leagues, fall basketball and playoffs all along the way, it was a year long sport and the competition was at a very good level at the time in the area. WNBA teams like the Detroit Shock sponsored our AAU teams, D1 College Teams like Michigan State held team camps for the High School Teams and there were invite-only individual camps that you needed multiple coach recommendations to get into. So when I was recruited and signed up with RIT Basketball I knew the level of play I was immersed in early on had given me a good start. But although I loved the sport, I didn't choose RIT strictly for the sport. In fact, I had already accepted early admission prior to meeting with my coach for the first time. I was playing because it brought me a lot of joy.

Nevertheless, signing up as a student-athlete at RIT still remains one of the most challenging, high stress and rewarding experiences I've ever gone through. Several years prior to my freshman year start the RIT Women's Basketball Team had only won one game. Yes, you are reading that right, 1 win in 24 tries. It was one of the most losing programs in NCAA history. Trying to recruit a plethora of female basketball players to a private technical school didn't help the cause. For instance, Engineering was one of the largest schools on campus and the ratio for guys to girls at the time was about 8:1. The girls used to say, the odds are good, but the goods are odd (that was not referring to basketball). So, with those odds how many stellar female basketball players do you think you'll find?

Anyway, I knew the statistics going into the program, but I didn't care. The freshman class had 6 solid recruits, we had a new coach and none of the baggage of constantly losing like the previous teams. Our coach was incredibly tough (with a background of winning at a high level) and her expectation was high to say the least. I still remember the day I got the pre-season workouts in the mail prior to freshman year and a 30+ page document arrived with track and weight workouts I had never heard of. Who names a running workout Fartlek? Come on.

That first year we tied the school record for wins and won 10. This was a huge feat considering the history of the program and the toughness of the competition we faced. I broke my hand in the midst of that 10th game that we won (and kept it hidden until a few days after), but had to sit out the two remaining games of the season. Thus, we each had a taste of success at that point, but had not yet made it over the hump.

It's hard to really describe the basketball years at RIT at that time to people that were not on the team. People would be hard pressed to believe what our team went through. Over the years it was a constant struggle to beat the record. The ups and downs were plenty with unforeseen injuries and losing new recruits that saw the intensity of the program and chose not to stay. There was the low of going through a 7-game losing streak and the high of nearly beating the #2 ranked school in the country, but still not making it to the promised land. There was potential and the weight of expectation. In addition, there was the mental strain of practicing sometimes 3 times per day, 6am workouts, long bus rides across the state, all while trying to obtain an engineering degree at a top academic program and simultaneously trying to figure out what you want to do with the rest of your life. Small tasks. I also can't tell you how many times I woke up to the nightmare of hearing my coach yell "get on the line" as the precursor to a running drill of 100+ sprints. If I'm honest, every year when I went home for the summer I thought about quitting. I was not on a scholarship. We were still a losing team and there was no glory of being a women's college basketball player at the time. The stands weren't packed, and all of us on the team just played because we loved the sport. There was only the unfinished business of breaking the record and not wanting to let my teammates down.

I still remember the day my senior year when I had the feeling it was all worth it. I was co-captain that year and our team, which had 4 seniors that had been on the journey since the start of the 4-year affair, had finally broken the win record at the time with 14. The program had never made it to post-season. It was our last home game and we were playing the #1 team in the league that we needed to beat in order to make it to the playoffs for the first time in our school's history. I remember walking into the locker room and being flooded with memories; the weekly weigh-ins to make sure we did not divert from our workout regimen during holiday breaks, the "hell week" practices with just running and no basketballs, the long

multi-hour locker room talks after a loss to figure out what

went wrong, the timed miles and track workouts in the

wee hours of the morning, the curfews for pre- and post-

season, and yet at that moment it all seemed worth it. No

matter what we had accomplished something. We had

survived and we were not broken.

The final game was tough though. It was a back and

forth battle, but with two minutes left each one of the

seniors did something that contributed to the win that day.

Jackie, our sharpshooter, hit two free throws without a

warmup. Jenna, our steady point guard, stole a pass that

led to Rama, the all-around player, making an incredible

left handed layup, and I hit a shot with the clock winding

down. We won that day and no one can ever take that

away from our team. It was a four-year mental and

physical challenge with an intensity level that is hard for

me to articulate, but through the ups and downs, we

persevered for years and we did it. The lesson of if you

work hard and stick with it, you will prevail is one I will

always carry with me.

Chapter 5

Inter-Conference Barbecue ...A Joke That Actually Happened

Through the stress and intensity of playing college basketball at an elite academic school, there were also plenty of good times. I will always share a bond with the friends that I made during that whole experience and could regale you with ridiculous stories that would shock you. However, there was one joke my senior year that all of a sudden became very real and it showed me that no matter how outrageous something is, it's possible to make it happen.

My good friend, Jackie, and I had often joked about getting to know the players in the conference by having a barbecue. What better way to get to know the stars of the league than by bonding over hot dogs, hamburgers, limbo and potato sack races. In our hearts, we wanted to make this a reality, but didn't know how to get the message across. Fortunately for us though the opportunity to speak at a banquet for a yearly local basketball tournament fell into our laps. Every year there was a Chase Bank sponsored tournament with at least 10 schools from the area that competed in a week long high energy tournament. Every year a captain from each school would give a speech at the banquet before the tournament commenced. Lucky for Jackie and I, it was my turn to speak this year which meant it was the perfect opportunity to turn our joke into a reality.

The crowd at the banquet had to be over 200. The room was filled with many coaches and players I respected. The typical captain's speech to this formally dressed crowd usually lasted two minutes or less with the same message of thank you and good luck. However, in my first real speech to an audience of this size, I knew I had one mission and one mission only: present the barbecue idea and hope I'm not dragged off the stage by the tournament directors, school director and my coach. The following speech took place in January of 2007:

"(Taps mic) Is this thing on? Sorry, I've always wanted to do that. Hello everyone, I didn't trip on the way up, so we're already off to a good start. This is my 4th Chase Banquet and every year each of the captains up here usually goes through a list of thank yous; typically Chase Bank, the honorees for the night and so on. However, I think there's a group we tend to forget ....the chefs. I know I come here every year for the food. As a college student living off of baloney and Easy Mac if I could get a free meal, it's a good deal. I mean every year we get free pasta, free cookies. I'm not going to lie I've taken more than one over the past three years, I'm sorry coach. If

anyone did not receive a cookie from the years 2003-2006.

I'll take the heat for those cookies.

Now that I have the microphone I'd like to share the idea of having an Inter-Conference Barbecue (gasps from the crowd) ...that girl over there wants a barbecue (points to crowd member). Basically, we'll all go to a park, we'll have hamburgers, we'll have hot dogs, we'll play bocce. We'll have a good ole fashioned potato sack race between the teams. The top seeded teams can bring the chips and the dip and the lower seeded teams can bring the meat. Fortunately, this year RIT Women's Basketball can get away with bringing Fritos and cheese puffs as opposed to Ball Park Franks. 7 and 3. Seriously, this is a great tournament, it's one of my favorite tournaments, sometimes it's the only tournament we go to each year, but there are some fine players and coaches and programs in this room and it's been a pleasure playing against all of you. So, thanks again and best of luck to all of the teams. "

And then I dropped the mic. Just kidding, I didn't drop the mic. It was attached to the stand. It was just one of those moments, where I took a chance. I was scared the entire night as I waited to go to the podium. I imagine I was sweating outrageously because I did not know how it would be received. And in the video there is a woman to my right who doesn't crack a smile. Regardless, there were a smattering of laughs throughout the crowd, and following the speech multiple players throughout the tournament came up to me and asked "when are we going to have a barbecue?".

So, when people want a barbecue, you have to give them a barbecue. The demand was there and after the season, Jackie and I set forth a plan to turn our joke into a reality. We had gained the email addresses of a few players in the joint training rooms before some of our remaining games. We had identified these people as team liaisons who we would communicate the details to as well as their coaches. We scouted several park locations to find the ideal spot and created a proposal for our athletic director to sponsor part of the event. We had a budget (which included having both of our fathers cook the hots and hams that day). I apparently had a potato sack contact and acquired the materials necessary for that event. We even raised some money and food for a local homeless shelter. And when it all came together, we had 4 full teams represented at that barbecue. We had a karaoke jam complete with Britney Spears classics, limbo contests, a football punting contest (where I most certainly pulled a Charlie Brown and missed the football completely). In addition to the great turnout, Jackie and I also had ICB t-shirts, beautiful hand-painted ceramic party favors, business cards (because who doesn't want a card that says you're the co-president of the Inter-Conference Barbecue), and finally, the school's local news team was there to capture the event on film.

If you had told me at the beginning of the season that our joke would have actually happened, I may have laughed in your face and told you to please leave the gym. But it happened and I'm glad that it did. The moral of the story is it's okay to take a chance. If you have an idea, then share it and create a plan to make it happen. If you believe in something, no matter how ridiculous it may seem, just go for it!

Chapter 6

What Does an Engineer Do Again? ... The Technical Problem Solver

RIT is a unique university. It is home to nine academic colleges. The majority of the colleges are devoted to engineering, computing and science, but RIT also provides fine arts and photography programs. Therefore, you have students with both the left and right brain type thinking all merged on one campus. Basically you have "the freaks and the geeks" in addition to the National Technical Institute for the Deaf (NTID) which is the largest technical school for students with hearing impairments comprising nearly 10% of the campus. Thus, there is an awkward mingling of calculators, cameras and interpreters all sharing the same snow covered campus.

I was in the 5-engineering year program, and at the time, the school was on the quarter system, which means you have 10 weeks to sink or swim plus 1 week of finals. This is intense, ladies and gentlemen. The first year for me was a bit of a blur. It really was all about survival. However, what wasn't blurry was when I got mono from my roommate the ninth week of the final quarter that first year. I had made the mistake of sharing cereal bowls with her, but I just couldn't help it. I loved Frosted Flakes and she had the tableware. My hand cast had just been taken off and I was cleared to play basketball again when I was diagnosed with mononucleosis. For those of you not familiar it's a common virus among teens and young adults (typically 95% of the population is exposed to it at some point in their lives) that's spread through saliva. Many get it through kissing, I acquired it over a love of General Mills breakfast cereals.

Mono basically requires a lot of bedrest typically for a month to get well. You become extremely tired with little to no appetite, and even after the first month, you're still exhausted 1-3 months later. Typically those suffering from mono lose weight. Funny enough, I actually gained weight on mono because my appetite came back and I started eating trays of delicious brownies, but was too exhausted to exercise or really move any portion of my body. In addition to the weight gain, I had acquired mono at the most crucial point of the school year and had to miss a week and a half of class. All that was left to do was shoot death stares at my roommate. I would have thrown left over Cocoa Puffs at her, but I just didn't have the energy. I was faced with the choice of going home and taking incompletes for my classes, or staying and somehow making up over a week's worth of work in my classes in the most crucial time of the quarter. Since I was stubborn and the thought of moving still seemed exhausting I decided to forge ahead with staying on campus and ended up pulling three all-nighters in a row to make up for the work I had missed. I somehow survived the all nighters, so the only thing left to do was to turn in a project in the morning and take the last of my finals at noon. I decided to "rest my eyes" for a bit only to wake up to the clock saying 12:43pm. I had made the classic mistake and mixed up the AM/PM on the alarm clock. I did the only thing I could think of and called my father. He gave me the sage advice of "run to class". In my pjs, flip flops and glasses I ran the sprint of my life, first throwing my project at the furthest building from the dorms and then bursting into the second half of my 2-hour final. The teacher had no mercy and I was forced to take the test in less than half the time. I learned a lot that day. First, always have a backup alarm. Second, I really should not have risked harm to my spleen and further damage to my body with the stress I was putting on my system. I do seem to recall feeling like my organs hurt following that week. Lastly and perhaps most crucially, it's better to eat the cereal right out of the box. Why risk it? Just pour the milk right in there and call it a day.

My next years at RIT were a little more steady. No known viruses came my way, but I still wasn't exactly sure what an engineer did despite completing a good amount of the course work. I understood the math and science of it, but how could I apply this to my toy engineer dreams? I received great advice from a professor about the Electrical and Mechanical sides of developing products and started working on an Independent Study where I could further explore this. I also began taking Industrial Design (ID) classes to get a different perspective of the toy making or consumer products process. It was a bit nerve wracking at first because I immediately felt as though "one of these things is not like the other" upon entering the ID classes. The students in the Industrial Design classes had talent and a far better sense of style while my claim to fame was basketball shorts and an assortment of mechanical pencils. However, it definitely gave me a greater appreciation for another way of looking at a product and has most certainly helped in my career working in multi-discipline teams. To explain, cross-functional teams in product development are traditionally comprised of people from very different worlds, with different jargons and a different approach to developing a product (i.e. Marketing, Industrial Design, Engineers, Graphic Artists, Manufacturers and so on). So, having experience in another thinking space made me see the product a little differently and I was not immediately dismissive (as others may have) of some of the ideas that came across my desk.

In my fourth year I started taking co-ops which are essentially paid internships. RIT required five 3-month blocks at the time for my program and it was a great opportunity to get a taste of the work world before leaving college. However, I also took it as a way to figure out what I did not want to do. I took a strategic approach to my co-ops and diversified them to experience multiple types of engineering. I completed two blocks of traditional engineering at a gas & electric company. I worked on the gas side, and I can assure you, they were already familiar with my retinue of gas jokes. I then tried my hand at research engineering by working for one of my professors to support a book he was writing at the time. Proceeding that experience, I landed the coveted co-op at Fisher-Price--the toy company of my dreams. My experience lasted three months and it felt completely in line with what I wanted to do in my life. However, being the competitive person that I am, I needed to do something to separate

myself from the other candidates whom which I would be

competing against for full-time jobs when school ended.

With every co-op experience, I tried to give something

back to the companies I worked for, whether it was

creating a manual for the incoming co-ops or some sort of

learning guide for speeding up the adjustment process

from school to work. This stuff was good, but it wasn't my

golden ticket. I immediately thought to myself what would

Willy Wonka do? When that didn't work, I figured I'd go

to Australia for my last co-op.

Chapter 7

Australia ....No, I Will not Throw that on the Barbie

I'm not sure when my fascination with Australia started. Maybe it was due to a childhood crush on the Australian Tennis Player, Patrick Rafter. Who knows? All I know is that I always wanted to go there, so why not make my final co-op in my last quarter of school an internship in Australia that would give me international experience and help set me apart from the other job candidates after college.

Since no one in my program had gone to Australia for a co-op at the time, it took about a year to get it approved with the Dean of the College as well as to find a reputable placement service for jobs and living. When all was said and done, I acquired a product development job working at ASDM or Advanced Surgical Design and

Manufacture, and I would be living with a woman and her 18 year-old son in Cremorne, a suburb of Sydney. Having only been out of the country to Canada, I knew this would be a life-changing experience or, at the very least, would provide me with a good tan? No?

I spent a quarter of school living with my grandma to save money for the trip and before I knew it I was off on a 21-hour flight (with no sleep) and headed down under. I was not in Kansas or Niagara Falls anymore.

The Aussie son had plenty of questions about America. In particular, he kept asking me about the "Crips and Bloods" gangs in L.A. I informed him the only gangs I knew of were the Jets and the Sharks from Westside Story. I told him "in America, we settle disputes with dance-offs." Then he asked me what there was to do in Delaware? I sidestepped that question and decided it was time to go to work.

Work was interesting. There were six engineers in the office and a manufacturing facility on the bottom floor. My assignment was to design the surgical plate that is implanted in patients for fractured clavicles. For a real-world application when rugby players inevitably break their clavicles in battle, this plate is implanted for about 6 months until the fracture heals and then the plate is removed. It was the kind of project where upon initial assignment, you think it will be way too much responsibility. I remember my first week being given a stack of books the size of encyclopedias. The reading assignment may have been due to the fact that only one computer in the office had access to the internet. Yes, one, like the number of wins the RIT Women's Basketball Team had in 2002. Nevertheless, I complied and filled my days reading up on the ever-exciting topic of clavicle implants.

Everything was new out here for me. That included getting to know the transportation system. On my first day using public transportation I inevitably traveled 30 minutes on a bus headed in the wrong direction. It included getting used to the local wildlife. The birds or Kookaburras sounded like whining monkeys. Then there was getting used to the local jargon:

- Bloak = Jerk or goofball (man)
- Dodgy = Crappy/Shady
- Uni = College
- That's Alright = You're Welcome
- Tomaaato = Tomato
- Lolli = Candy
- Holiday = Vacation
- Shocker = Horrible
- Heaps = A lot
- Bombag = Fannypack

- Bird = Female

- Barbie = Barbecue

- Swim costumes = Swimsuits

- No worries = No problem

- Mum = Mom

- Blitz it = great job

- Cheek = Joke

- Ice Blocks = Popsicle minus the stick

- Fair dinkem mate = really man

- Bloody oath = yeah right

- Good on you = well done

- Jinks = Gee

- Crivvens = Gee

- Scratcher = Bed

- Moo = Mouth

- Jakie = Alcoholic

- Muckle = Large

- Gadgie = Guy (or bloak)

- Dub = Puddle

- Bobblers = drinking fountain

Of course, I did the touristy things and went to all the highlights like catching a show at the Sydney Opera House, going to museums and parks, seeing a rugby game and even hanging out with an Aborigine (what's left of them) in the Blue Mountains. I took a picture with good old Goombar, the loincloth wearing, Smokey the Bear-esque Aborigine, then tried to convince my family it was my new boyfriend.

The weeks flew by with work and fun and before I knew it I was in my last week in Australia. A few weeks prior I had asked the CEO of the company I was working with if I could go to a surgery with him. In addition to my company making the surgical equipment, it had surgeons that would implant what was created as well. My last

Monday in Australia, I found myself in the operating room for three knee surgeries. I had all of the scrubs on including a face mask. The head surgeon was supposed to be the top knee surgeon in Australia. He finished one knee in about 40 minutes. It can usually take surgeons up to two hours. The first knee surgery was for an 80 year old man whose leg was crooked. The next two were for an obese woman whose knees were knocked or turned inward.

The CEO actually assisted in on the surgeries. He was a surgeon, an engineer and the owner of a business, but was also the type of guy that would joke around a little too much. On the car ride over he asked me my last name and then followed it up with asking if my mom was a real estate agent in New York. I then quickly followed up with, "Why….are you my father?" His response was, "That's why I never answer the phone on Father's Day." And with that my internship concluded.

I said my goodbyes to my Australian family, for they had been incredibly kind to me and I also got the chance to meet and hangout with the other siblings who were just as wonderful. Before I left I agreed to throw the "footy" or rugby football around with the Aussie son in the yard one last time. I was a little too determined to catch the ball and ended up splitting my pants, a proper fitting (or lack thereof?) for the ending of my first international experience.

Chapter 8

Toy Dream Come True (Fisher-Price)

I was in the Sydney Airport on my way back to the states and checking my email at a kiosk when I found out there was a position available at Fisher-Price for a Product Development Engineer. The timing could not have been better. I was weeks away from RIT's graduation and knew that going back to my old room in Michigan at my parents' house replete with Michael Jordan and Austin Powers posters was my last option. Although continuous, delicious home cooked meals was tempting, it was time to keep moving forward. So I packed up my Mini-Me poster and headed to the job interview.

I arrived at the East Aurora, NY Fisher-Price Headquarters and went through a day long interview process with all of the engineering managers for the different toy groups. I didn't land all of my jokes that day, but I did land the job and started my career in the baby toy department (developing toys for Birth to 3 years old). I had worked in the baby gear department (developing products that would physically hold newborns in some instances) for my internship, so I had an idea of the challenges ahead. However, I think with any first real job everyone has the same feeling. You are confident because you secured the position, but concurrently there's a bit of fear that you may screw up. The biggest challenge for me was knowing that there were questions I needed to ask, but not even knowing how to articulate those questions at first. Many companies adopt the sink or swim approach with new employees and you are thrown into the grind with little transition. Fortunately, I was surrounded by marketing, design and engineering wizards employed by the company for 10, 20, 30 and even 40 years who were great teachers throughout my time at Fisher-Price. When you actually meet the creators behind some of your childhood toys, it is tough not to be in awe of their talent and creativity. It was like I was surrounded by Santa's genius everyday and I did not want to disappoint.

I had a Fisher-Price Power Wheels for one day when I was nine, arguably a few years past the recommended age grade for the toy. I was definitely way too old and big (physically) to have this toy. As I sat in the truck, my knees approached my chin and I encroached on the second seat next to me, but I didn't care. I finally had some wheels to make the trip back and forth to the mailbox an easier one. Unfortunately, there was something wrong with the horn and we had to take it back to the store to get it replaced. Here is where I committed one of the biggest transgressions of my life. Out of the corner of my eye, I saw a giant stuffed ninja turtle and was entranced. I foolishly opted to get the $2 carny quality stuffed toy in place of that fine piece of Fisher-Price engineering. As I told this story to my new boss, who used to run the Power Wheels Department, I knew I had some work to do in order to make up for my past mistake.

One of my greatest contributions at Fisher-Price outside of my daily hijinks of photoshopped images and collaboration on the creation of 80+ toys, was creating the I.D.C. (Inter-Department Challenge). No, we did not go to a park and have potato sack races. At our holiday party I organized and MC'd an event with Minute to Win It games, which were one-minute challenges with everyday items that usually involved stacking something (blocks, cups, etc.), balancing something (plates, cans, etc.) or throwing something (ping pong balls, rubber bands, etc.).

Many times the games were Marketing vs. Design vs. Engineering to mirror the challenges in product development, but it all came down to good old fashioned fun. There was also a prize box filled with Dollar Store items! It was this type of environment where there was the freedom to enact non-traditional events like this in a corporate arena where I was able to create and think a little differently. Thus, my time at the company will always be a memorable one, where I learned not only how to develop products and focus on the consumer and their needs, but also how to develop an environment for a successful team.

Chapter 9

The China Experience ...Learning the Manufacturing Ropes

As part of the training at the time, Fisher-Price sent its new engineers for a one-month stay in Tijuana, Mexico and a one-month stay in mainland China to learn about and tour different manufacturing facilities. Having just come off my Australia high, I was eager to travel again and readily accepted these ventures.

The first trip to Tijuana was an experience to say the least. I traveled with three other employees and we had to stay in San Diego because it was too dangerous to stay in Tijuana. We would walk or take the trolley to the border past the beggars and drug mules everyday. Aside from the daily border crossing experiences and occasionally seeing a truck filled with men wielding what looked like machine guns, the people I met were fantastic and there was a true sense of family with everyone you would meet in the plant. It was a bit of an adjustment to get accustomed to daily hugs with co-workers at the start and finish of each day. The standard American handshake greeting I offered would not satisfy anyone in the office, but before I knew it I was immersing myself in the daily embraces.

I adopted the Jim Carrey "Yes Man" philosophy and found myself agreeing to try anything including tasting a cow's tongue taco, being serenaded by a mariachi band at Los Remedios cantina and accepting an offer to play in a local golf tournament where I lost miserably. All in all, Mexico was a success filled with new experiences and tomfoolery. With Tijuana behind me, the next stop was a tour in mainland China.

China was filled with many surprises. The first being when I walked into a restroom and saw the hole in the ground. This non-western toilet certainly presented some challenges to a newbie of the Asian continent. As I stood looking at the toilet situation for several minutes to figure out my approach, I was often bamboozled by the proper angles and stance to use. And yet the biggest challenge for me in China was not the 10+ factories that we visited, but getting accustomed to the food which was much different than the Americanized Chinese food I was used to.

The meats typically had large bones left in them which made it difficult to pick up with chopsticks. The chopsticks were really my greatest nemesis there. Every meal it was me vs. the chopsticks…and I tended to lose those battles. Oh, how I pined for a fork. I would wonder what it was doing, who it was with. I would wonder if it was thinking about me the way I was thinking about it, tenderly spiralling spaghetti noodles around its perfectly engineered tines. Amongst the delicacies I tasted in China were shark fin dumplings, duck wings, rabbit (I'm sorry Wilbur, you were a good pet) fish with the head and fins still in the bowl, chicken cartilage on a stick, octopus balls and other miscellaneous unidentified meats. Each meal was a test to my system to see if it would be rejected or accepted. At one point in the trip, I was faced with a hot bowl of mystery meat. I wanted to be courteous to the culture and try everything before me, but the spongy white octopus balls from 10 minutes ago were not sitting well. I did the only thing I knew how to do. I hid the meat in front of me in a napkin and placed it on the window sill beside me. This wasn't my proudest moment and I'm sure the waitress had quite a surprise when she found the 10 or so rolled up meat napkins at the base of the window, but it was deemed necessary for my survival and I was able to live another day in China.

It wasn't just all work and all food for the trip. The office I was with had arranged nightly sporting activities after the long days at the plants as an opportunity for everyone to get to know each other better. I considered this my personal Olympics unbeknownst to anyone I was competing against. It is worth noting that these after-work activities tended to draw crowds. For one thing, I am a tall, non-Asian, gangly armed gal in the middle of China that was engaging in a plethora of activities around the city. I tended to stand out. We played tennis and I did my best Serena Williams impression adding grunts after every ball hit, but the joke was lost in translation. Later in the week we moved on to ice skating which took place in the middle of a five-story mall. This was my first experience on ice skates and my goal was not to fall. I still recall the look on the lady's face when I gave her my EURO shoe size. She stared at me in sheer amazement like I had uttered a number that never existed. Soon after finding a pair of acceptable ogre-sized skates, I was gliding across the ice like the love child of Tonya Harding and Brian Boitano. The medal count finished at 5-1 USA as I lost a round of Badminton despite having warmed up with the Rocky theme song and wind sprints to get loose before the match.

The trip to China was winding down and all that was left to do was exit Customs. I accidentally got in the "Chinese Nationals" line, but was re-directed when I felt a gentle tap on my shoulder by a tiny women that aggressively pointed to the "Foreigners" line. It was time to go. A trip not to be forgotten with much learned along the way, but little did I know this would be the first of a handful or trips to China and thus more opportunities to redeem myself against my greatest foe, the chopstick.

Picture Gallery

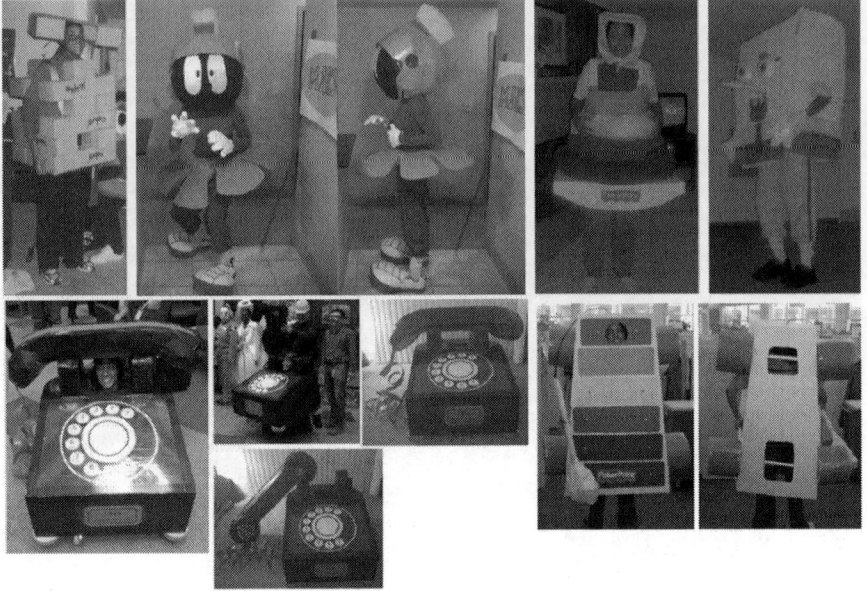

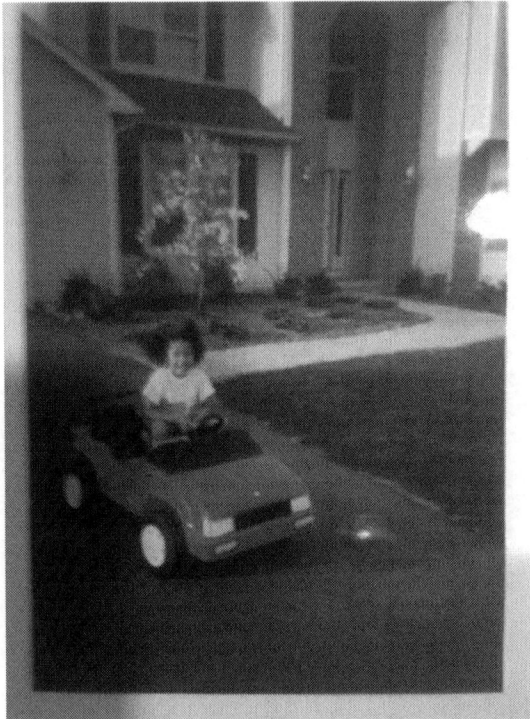

Chapter 10

Marathons ....Why am I Running Again?

After coming back from Australia, finishing school, starting a new job and just prior to leaving for Mexico and China for the manufacturing training I figured I should take it easy for bit .... and train for a marathon.

I never considered myself a runner and frankly I was not sure if I would physically and mentally be able to complete a marathon (flashes back to "chub year" period and not being able to complete one pull up on the Presidential Fitness Test in gym class), but since I was done with basketball I needed something to replace the years of training I was conditioned to doing. I had played competitive basketball all year round since the age of 10 and was beginning to miss the competition. Naturally I found myself getting in treadmill races with people at the gym to see who could stay on the machine the longest.

I selected the Detroit Marathon as my first race in the Fall of 2009. It had some cool features. You ran in and out of Canada, the runner size was in the tens of thousands, and there was an underwater mile portion of the course where you ran through a tunnel. I created a five month plan to accomplish this feat. I methodically went through this plan, but of course there were a few ups and downs along the way. For instance, I learned that waffles before a run was a bad choice and that running along a two-lane highway required an ID bracelet so your body could be easily identified in the event you were struck. Solid tips for a newbie runner.

After months of consistently running each week and following a plan (not knowing if it was the right one), race day was here and, by golly, it was cold outside. The race started with a temperature of 32 degrees Fahrenheit and I was surrounded by nearly 20,000 runners. Luckily the fear I had going into the race was enough to warm me up until the start gun went off. I started off fast, not sure if it was to get out of the cold or maybe I just had to pee and wanted to get inside, but my pace was a little faster than I trained for. I figured I could keep going at this pace, but after awhile I did the worst thing you could do as a long distance runner ....think. When you're running for so long you're trying to distract yourself from thinking about how long you have left. Your body can physically do it with the months of training you have put in, but somewhere along the race your mind shifts like a 10 year old on Halloween when you realize you have to wait for your parents to check your candy before you can devour anything. You desperately want to get to the candy, but the struggle and mental fortitude needed to wait through other meals and activities before your tiny hands can grasp victory is all too real.

Around the 18th mile, my thoughts moved past French fries and wondering whether or not the people next to me had acquired the latest bout of swine flu. My focus waned and I began thinking about the many miles I had left. My pace began to slow and women with strollers and babies seemed to pass me. Additionally, I had run out of water and gels from my running belt. When I got to mile number 22 I started to hallucinate. I didn't stop. I wouldn't stop, but I definitely felt like I was outside of my body watching myself run. It was a weird feeling to say the least, but I saw the finish line soon and stupidly sprinted to the end only to lose all feeling in my legs when I stopped just past the line. I finished in 4 hours and 5 minutes. Mission accomplished? Unfortunately, the celebration of the day was cut a little short, when we learned that 3 runners died that day during the half marathon. It was an anomaly for races, but it definitely impacted the mood of the race.

After the race and subsequent international trips for work I decided to take a little workout hiatus and began graduate school in 2010. I hung up my running shoes for a bit only to lace them back up in 2012 for the Chicago Marathon after I had finished graduate school. I ran for one reason only that time, to prove that it wasn't a fluke (a foolish reason I suppose), but I finished about a minute off my first race time. I didn't necessarily enjoy running, but I started training for the next one so I could break the 4 hour mark. A few months into training during a 16 mile run I got to mile 8 again and just stopped. I wasn't thinking about french fries or swine flu, but the thought that crossed my mind that time was the very same thought I had at the start of all of those other races, 'why am I running again?'

I walked the rest of the way home and stopped training. I personally needed something else ….something that was more fulfilling for me…

Chapter 11

A Wee Wee...Europe Trip / Masters

Somewhere between marathons and China, I decided to go to graduate school. I had been wrestling with the idea for a while now and was trying to be thoughtful in the program that I chose. I considered MBA programs, and even sat in on an Executive Master's program at the University of Rochester as they covered the exciting topic of Accounting. However, I ultimately decided on the Masters of Product Development Program at my alma matter, Rochester Institute of Technology. The program was just what I was looking for. It had a combination of engineering, manufacturing and business where I could benefit immediately and apply what I was learning directly to my current job as a Product Development Engineer. There was one kicker though. The school was an hour and a half drive from my work. 2-3 times per week after a full day's work I drove 1.5 hours to a 3-hour class and then 1.5 hours back home to crash immediately at my apartment. Needless to say, there was an increase of caffeine intake during this 2-year grind. The schedule was demanding, but I genuinely looked forward to my classes. There is something about being on a college campus that I've always enjoyed. Maybe it's the feeling of hope on campus and rarely do you run into jaded individuals, which is more common in the corporate world. I could not wait to get to class for the discussions and learn from the other students who typically had at least 5 years' work experience (as required by the program). I had been admitted to the program with a little less work experience, but my additional year of co-op and academic background with the school allowed me to enter the M.S. a bit early.

I made great discoveries during this time period in my life. One class in particular, Excellence in Product Development, largely impacted my life trajectory. The professor, Tim had a great way of simply making you think--everything from what you currently were getting out of your work to evaluating your workplace to determining what was needed from a work environment. This made me take a hard look at the direction I wanted my career to go in and also planted a seed that just because I had landed my dream job initially, didn't mean that I had to stay there forever. I could stray from Tom Hanks movies and find a picture to inspire my life other than the movie, Big. Perhaps Jumanji? I do like a good board game. I also became fascinated with the topic of Organizational Behavior. I was constantly curious about and enthralled by the different roles in an organization, what motivates people and the impact of environment on the efficiency and effectiveness of a company. I plowed through my second stint at RIT as a metaphorical sponge trying to soak up everything that I could. I was drained ….no… soaked by graduation and wanted to have a little fun and celebrate what I had accomplished. So I planned a whirlwind 2.5 week tour of a few cities in Europe.

I started my trip in London with a goal of getting to the fish and chips. I arrived at my "flat" aka apartment in Notting Hill and managed to get in a few sights the first couple of days. I walked across London's Bridge and surprisingly, it did not fall down. Later, I hopped on the TUBE subway system and made my way to Pollack's Toy Museum. I dropped the "I work at a Toy company" line in the hopes of getting some sort of discount or continued conversation with the man behind the counter, but no such luck. I shuffled and skedaddled across town to Shakespeare's Globe theater to take in a play. I grabbed what I thought was a great ticket hugging the stage of the Tempest play only to learn that a lot of British actors spit when they perform. After the first saliva-spraying act, I headed out and took a bus to the city of Cambridge to enjoy bike rides in the countryside.

I continued moving and made my way to Paris. Of course, I took in all of the museums which unfortunately included getting sick in front of the Mona Lisa (she was looking at me the whole time). I continued to see sites until it was time to hop on a night train to the next location, Madrid. The 13 hours of awkward exchanges in the train cabin with 3 others that didn't speak English should have been my first clue that I would struggle with the language barrier here. What I learned is that my 8th and 9th grade Spanish classes were not proving beneficial here. The only thing I could do was recite the happy birthday song and not everyone likes to be greeted with

"Feliz cumpleanos a ti….". This was only able to get me to and out of a bullfight in Madrid. I went to a bullfight and my naivety showed on full display here because I did not know they killed the bull in the ring. I had made it to the Coliseum, Las Ventas with the hopes of taking in a cultural sporting event. As people cheered voraciously for the bull to be stabbed repeatedly I figured this was not the place for me. I left before the end and frantically looked for the exit. Unfortunately, I chose the wrong door and when I looked down I was standing over a trail of blood from the dead bull they had just dragged out from the ring. Needless to say, it was rice for dinner.

I kept moving and took over 25 hours of night trains in a few days back to Paris, then to Rome (the only night train route possible) and discovered that consuming an entire pizza on your own in Rome is socially acceptable. My goodness, the food! I had found the motherload and stationed myself at several restaurants filling my days and gullet with delicious Italian cuisine. I made it to the Colosseum, the Vatican and all the other notorious sites. Unfortunately, I had one bad encounter with a museum agent where I was treated poorly before entering the museum and thought about causing an international incident and revealing a "Free Amanda Knox" t-shirt, but figured it was time to keep moving.

I took another night train back to Paris and capped my trip by landing tickets to both women's semi-final French Open Tennis matches aka Serena Williams destroying the women's field of tennis players. Prior to the match, Serena happened to walk by me. I instantly turned into a teenage girl in the presence of Justin Bieber and shrieked "Serena, you're my favorite athlete". She turned and smiled in my direction and I couldn't be happier. I ruined the moment by paparazzi-ing her picture, but none of that mattered as she won that day and the next with

ease. Finally after countless hours on night trains hopping

all over Europe, it was time to head back home. I had seen

a lot and taken in the sites that I had read about in school

growing up. I was glad to be home because the trip was

exhausting, but I still had an itch to see and do more…

Chapter 12

No PhD (the Start of Lecturing) and Costa Rica (48 Hrs. Notice)

In addition to all of the traveling, school, running and work I had also started volunteering with students in my free time; everything from being a Calculus tutor at a summer program at Kettering University to developing multiple STEM (Science, Technology, Engineering and Math) programs for the University of Buffalo, to going back to RIT to speak to the incoming freshman classes, and even guest lecturing at Boston College to share another career avenue of engineering. It was all very exciting, rewarding and gave me a great opportunity to test out my new jokes. But joking aside, I truly enjoyed volunteering. There was something about the challenge of engaging an audience and guiding students in one way or another that appealed to me. I remember during one class I could tell that the students were not awake yet or just weren't into what I was saying yet. Knowing I had to do something that would grab their attention, I blurted out, 'Who thinks this toy infant table (that I had brought as a sample) will break if I stand on it?". Instantly, the students eyes began to widen and I could see their thought bubbles popping up. Luckily for me, I had just done a load bearing test on a majority of the Fisher-Price tables that week and I knew that even though I had an extra slice of cake that morning, the table was not going to break if I stood on it. So I jumped on the table and of course it didn't break. The students were instantly engaged and it was on to the next part of the lecture as they sat up a little more in their chairs.

I had come from a family of teachers and had always thought of the teacher as one of the noblest professions. At this point in my life, I began thinking about pursuing a career as a professor, but of course I knew I needed to climb the PhD ladder first (and what a mighty ladder it would be!). I started investigating schools and thinking about what I wanted to study, knowing that with each next level of education, the focus would narrow. There were only a handful of Product Development Masters programs in the country, so the odds of finding a PhD program that I liked in that field within the states was slim. Therefore, I shifted my thinking to Organizational Behavior in the Sociology or Business programs. I loved the topic in my Master's program, and having worked in corporations for a bit, I could see the obvious benefit of focusing on this area of study.

I hunted down a former Sociology professor to seek his counsel. He advised me that the possibility of teaching jobs in this area would be heavily dependent on the name of the school from which I received my PhD. I focused on

5 top schools known for these programs: (1) Northwestern, (2) University of Chicago, (3) Stanford, (4) Harvard and (5) Cornell. I methodically went through the application processes, tracking down transcripts, studying and taking additional tests (GRE), gathering writing samples and trying to determine my future goals in the field of study. I was in knee deep and already starting to prepare myself for another five or more years of school. I had told no one about this pursuit except the professors whose recommendations I requested. I then submitted the paperwork and all that was left to do was wait. I was excited about the next chapter. I finally had a little more direction. I had learned a lot at Fisher-Price, but figured it was time for a shift in my career and a PhD program seemed like the right path.

It was the last week in February of 2014 where my fate was sealed. Every day for five days I received a rejection letter from those schools like clockwork. It was heartbreaking given it was the first time where I had worked hard for something, met the qualifications, and did not achieve the results I anticipated. I was lost with what to do next. I knew I needed to move on, but had no idea where to go. I took a week going over the applications to see where I had made any missteps, then started to reach out to current PhD students to see how their candidacy had taken shape. After months of this I decided to do the only thing I knew how to do .....go on a spontaneous international trip to clear my head. Within 48 hours I booked a trip to Costa Rica for a week. I still remember the email I sent my boss. The gist of the email was, my work is complete, headed to Costa Rica, be back next week. Not sure if I added a smiley face to the end of the email, but I'm sure it was implied.

I arrived in La Fortuna, Costa Rica and was staying in a cabin next to an active volcano (yes, I said an active volcano). I knew I had 3 minutes if it erupted and figured my Girl Scout training of yesteryear would leave me amply prepared. I'm certain I had a badge for volcano evacuation. While I was there I went on hikes, I soaked with strangers in one of many local hot springs and went rafting down the Peñas Blanca River. The river was so brown I knew that if I accidentally fell in my chances of getting the West Nile Virus (even though I was not in the West Nile target zone) would increase significantly.

I continued my daily adventures and ended up going horseback riding to some waterfalls, which may not sound like much at first. However, to appreciate the significance of this venture one must go back to the time of side pony hairstyles and Zach Morris from Saved By the Bell. The year was 1995 and it was time for a family vacation. The plan was to ride horses. Unfortunately, I was too short to ride the regular sized horses and too fat to ride a pony. Yes, you guessed it, this was during my chub years. What resulted from this 90s-failure, unbeknownst to my family who rode off into the sunset, was I got stuck in the stables washing the horse known as "Old Ben". Since then everytime I hear the word, "horse" I'm taken back to those hellish stables where dreams go to die. That is, UNTIL that day in Costa Rica. Redemption, my friends. I rode a horse named Miel, which I assume can be directly translated as Old Ben 2. Old Ben 2 was a spunky horse built for a solid 3-hour ride through the country stopping only for the occasional grass and for sightseeing at some amazing waterfalls. At these waterfalls, I passed on the opportunity to swim, but history was re-written that day for me and my horse memories will now always circle back on Old Ben 2 in Central America.

I was approaching my last adventure of the trip and of course had saved the best for last--zip lining through the rainforest. I wouldn't say I'm afraid of heights, but I'm definitely not comfortable with them. I said 'yes' to the adventure anyway because, I mean, how often are you in Costa Rica? Don't answer that for I am not sure of your ties to the international coffee trade. We trucked up a mountain to 12 lines each with varying lengths. The cables were about 55 meters high and the longest one was over 800 meters (unit conversion = that's a lot). It was just me and two guides and we were plugging along one line after another. I remember thinking the last time I was this scared was when I overslept for my DC Circuits final freshman year and had to sprint in my pjs midway through, but you already know about that. I zipped along that day while gravely speculating over the regulations for zip lines in Costa Rica. Nonetheless, I made it in one piece and headed back to the states with a newfound love of adventure. I also knew it was time to find another adventure work wise. I returned home, refreshed and refocused. The time was now and the search for the next stop would begin.

Chapter 13

From Baby Toys to Adult Toys (Brookstone)

The job search had begun and it was proving difficult to find a position that wasn't a lateral move and also appealed to me. At first I scoured the internet, searching for anything I could find, but with all Google job searches, there comes a point where you're not really getting anywhere. I had been out of the job search game for six years and wasn't sure what was the best approach. So, like a struggling maple syrup vendor, I decided to tap another resource. I went back to RIT and set up an appointment with the fabulous RIT Alumni Career Services Office who I had worked with previously when searching for interns or working at the school's Career Fair as a company representative. Thus, they guided me on my own job search approach and strongly recommended getting on LinkedIn. At this point, I had avoided all forms of social media like the plague. I was afraid of its mystical powers and wasn't sure I wanted to put myself out there. I had seen some of the permanent college basketball pictures that were out there of me online and couldn't risk another sweaty mishap pasted over the world wide web forever. Nevertheless, I started researching how to build a good LinkedIn profile and how to make myself stand out. Only after a few short weeks of daily working on the profile did the Senior Mechanical Engineer job at Brookstone pop onto my radar.

First, like many people, I had no idea Brookstone had a development team. I just knew of their awesome products and the mesmerizing sales people that lured you into their stores in the mall with flying objects, massage chairs, and other cool gadgets. Second, I couldn't believe my luck. This job looked exciting, it looked challenging and it was a move in the right direction. Literally, it was situated within reasonable driving distance to Boston, so I would have access to a few more things compared to my current location in the suburbs of Buffalo, New York. As I continued to weigh the plusses and minuses the only con was the idea of leaving my Fisher-Price family behind. In a way I had grown up with these people. I had made some great friends and I had learned so much about developing products the right way. I was indebted to them.

Fortunately, the Brookstone interview went well and I was offered a job a day or so after the interview. When the time came to part ways from the Toy World I dreaded the day. I had told no one about my job searching. I didn't like putting people in positions where they would have to keep something secret, so I kept the burden on myself. I'm sure many people had figured it out though, because over the previous week I had systematically taken my personal effects from my office. It was cleaner than the day I started. The days prior, I slowly collected my Mr. T Keychain that had a button that repeatedly played "I pity the fool". I packed up my FP Radio that my Uncle had found and saved for me that was a toy from the late 60s. Lastly, I took my company gift of the Tickle Me Elmo 10-year anniversary toy that I had skinned to see what the mechanism was underneath.

I planned a meeting with my boss and his superior at 8:05am. I knew based on the Company Handbook that it would be my last day. Although Brookstone wasn't a direct competitor of Fisher-Price, Brookstone still made some toys and based on the letter of the law in that Handbook, it was a conflict of interest and would be my last day surrounded by the colorful walls and toy covered cubicles of FP. As I handed in my letter, along with a list of my projects and their statuses I did my best to keep it together. Boy, was I nervous, but the meeting ended when I thanked both bosses for their support and was told to wait in my cubicle and not tell a soul until the HR Department had been notified and the paperwork had been sorted. I walked back to my desk and didn't tell anyone. Although people constantly came to my office asking what was going on due to the fact that I was in a closed-door meeting at the start of the day with 2 high ranking people in the department, I still kept my word and said I couldn't discuss anything at the moment. I waited hours until the new SVP of Product Development at the time asked to see me. We had a lovely, supportive conversation and he said I was welcome to come back to the company at any time. I went back to my office with still the directive to not say a word. Hours again passed and no new information was before me. Word had gotten out (not by me) and people began calling and stopping by. I heard from one of my bosses that the SVP of Product Development had said I now had the option to (a) stay at the company for 2 weeks (because they didn't think I would take any Intellectual Property) or (b) I could leave today and he would rescind his offer for me to come back to the company at a later date. I had already committed to my new company based on the Company Guidelines and was not going to cower to the situation I was being put in. I kindly retorted that this would be my last day, sent one last email to my friends at the company thanking them for making my toy dream come true. I grabbed my coat and walked to the HR Building. My boss sincerely apologized for the events of the day (that were out of his control), I filled out a few final documents, handed in my badge and said what goodbyes I could in the last remaining moments. It was an abrupt end to an overall lovely time with the company and people. However, it was time for a change and time to grow up and make the move from baby toys at Fisher-

Price to adult toys at Brookstone.

Chapter 14

Brazil ....Holy Poverty, Batman

Things were fine and dandy at Brookstone. I was amongst a very talented lab team that was responsible for designing and developing about 70% of the products that you see in the Brookstone stores. Everyone in the lab was incredibly hard working and put in a lot of hours. The jokes were plentiful and the team was solid. Here my engineering senses definitely were tickled by getting the chance to develop bluetooth speakers, headphones, footbaths, different types of massagers (yes, all types of massagers), app controlled devices and much much more. It was truly a Product Development Engineer's playground.

Halfway through my time at Brookstone, I had planned several months prior to go to Brazil. This was not my typical vacation. I wanted something a little different. I had worked and lived overseas in Australia, I had done the whole touristy backpackers Europe thing, and I had done the adventure thing in Costa Rica, but this time I wanted to try my hand at volunteering overseas. Volunteering had always been a part of my life, whether it was donating to the needy or participating in awareness events for different causes. Regardless of those volunteer experiences, it was my last year at RIT in my undergraduate years when I took a class called Social Inequality that sparked something in me. We had an assignment to write and experience different types of imbalances in society and I had chosen to visit a soup kitchen for the homeless. A family friend was heavily involved in this area and I found myself volunteering every Friday morning with her to go to this shelter run by 4 spry nuns in their 80s. They had the energy of meerkats and at the age of 21 I was just trying to keep up. The assignment had long since passed, but I felt the need to keep going. The soup kitchen experience stuck with me and years later I found a non-profit organization called Cross Cultural Solutions that had home bases in 10 different countries and combined volunteering, learning about the local culture as well as day trips for different international experiences. I chose Salvador, Brazil in a culture rich area called, Bahia (baaaa-he-a) where I used my vacation time to work at a homeless shelter (called Vo Flor) for kids.

There were a few language hurdles right at the beginning. I tried to learn Portuguese via Rosetta Stone before I left, but if you've ever ventured down the R-Stone path you quickly realize that there are over 600 lessons to complete. As the woman on the plane seat next to me from Miami to Salvador tried to speak to me in Portuguese, a wave of panic came over me as I remembered I had only completed language lessons 10 of 650 before I left. It didn't seem like the lady mentioned animals, colors or numbers, so, I mumbled something in Spanish and pondered how long I would be able to get by on "pequeno Portuguese".

I arrived at the place I would call home for the next few weeks which was a house situated across from a military area in the city. Upon arrival the Program Director gave us several instructions: (1) Do not turn left out of the home base, (2) Do not carry valuables, (3) If you do carry valuables then keep them in your pockets or bra (side note: the bra was not built to carry a Nikon Camera), (4) Do not flush the toilet paper (I'll leave the challenges that accompany that rule to your imagination), (5) Be careful. Then the instructor pointed to me and said, "You're the only one that could pass as Brazilian, until you open your mouth". "Thank you?" I retorted. The best part about the living situation was that I was sharing a room full of bunk beds with four 18 year old girls and what I learned during this trip is that my target audience for jokes is not 18 year old millennials.

I arrived at my assignment at Vo Flor and there were about 50 kids on day 1 that ranged in age from 2 to 12 yrs. old. It was run by an older woman in her 80s or possibly 90s who had been working at orphanages and daycare centers for years. The kids I came across were much like any kids you would find at a summer camp or day care center across the US. There was the kid that always cries, the kid you can't believe is so smart at his/her age, the kid that has a striking resemblance to Urkel, the group of 10 year old girls that can't bear to be separated from each other and the girl rocking the side pony tail wearing all purple with a little too much sass. However, there were some tough moments that hit home and clearly showed this was not the typical experience. On my first day, a table holding a broken TV fell on one boy (he was ok), one boy's father just died the previous morning and he wouldn't stop crying and the conditions were something that you just had to block out. I approached my first day the same as I did my first day of kindergarten. I made "munchies" (duck shaped origami) and paper planes to curry favor with the children.

To further detail my days, the usual suspects at Vo Flor each day included 3-6 high school aged boys that typically just did their own thing unless they tried to engage in conversation with me. They quickly realized that my smiles and head nods were code for I do not know what you're saying or they lost patience waiting for me to find the words in my English to Portuguese dictionary, so they soon dispersed. There were 4-5 girls that are in the 8-12 yr. old range that love to paint each other's nails. I came home one day with pink and purple nail polish all over my hands and took a solid 15 minutes to re-assess how I'd gotten to this point. I had made it through elementary, high school and college without pink nail polish and in one week at Vo Flor my hands were covered. After that there were 5-7 middle school aged boys that will play any game involving a ball or paper airplanes. Followed by 3-5 two year olds that love handing over urine soaked stuffed animals and who have been instrumental in improving my fitness out here. Then, there are 2 dogs. One that looks like a lion and one that remains tied up in the back room and heeds the same warning as The Beast from the Sandlot movie. Other than animals and kids, there were 2-3 ladies walking around besides Flor; her sister who is mentally challenged and typically has at least one episode in the morning, and another woman who is usually in the midst of hanging up her laundry in the play area. Finally, sometimes there's a group of adults in the back room that are learning to read and write in Portuguese. The house was fairly low key, but one amazing thing happened amongst the chaos. As I was leaving for the day, a random man dropped off a donation of toys and, what do you know, one was a product that I had a part in developing at Fisher-Price. The toy was built for batteries and I'm sure it will never see them at Vo Flor, but it was a cool moment that I'll always remember as the kids huddled around one of the many creations from FP and were enthralled by all of the features.

Aside from the chaos at the school, I had taken part in a few other activities that included a Futbol Game in a beautiful stadium situated in the middle of poverty. The crowd was like being in the student section of a Syracuse Basketball game, but with less orange and more drums. I saw a production called Bale Folclorico Da Bahia, which was a Portuguese / European / African inspired performance that had to be one of the most beautiful things I have ever witnessed. Then there was the Samba Lesson (yes, that's right, Samba Lesson), and if this was Dancing with the Stars I would have been voted off first. Samba is kind of like a combination of Zumba, Hip Hop and the Carlton Dance from the Fresh Prince of Bel-Air. Of course, I focused on the Carlton Dance portion. The instructor asked if I had played sports. I replied "basketball." She said "move your hips like in basketball". I replied, "I think I'd get some sort of personal foul if I moved my hips like that in basketball." Other activities included Portuguese language lessons each week and trying to learn Capoeira (dance fighting), which for me was like trying to learn how to walk again. The coordination needed between my arms and legs was something I wasn't prepared for, and my only previous work for this type of dance fight lesson was countless hours of watching West Side Story Jet/Shark street dance moves. (Side note: I know what you're thinking, how is it possible that this book has two West Side Story references?)

After a weekend trip to Rio to visit a family friend and see another part of Brazil I came back to my assignment and was faced with the harsh realities of seeing pictures of the block houses where some of the kids lived when they're not at Vo Flor. At which point, I immediately focused on a 5-part plan to Angelina Jolie these kids to the US. I thought better and as I was leaving / removing the kids from my suitcase, one of the women gave me a thank you note (in Portuguese) and a stuffed frog to always remind me of the kids.

As I was leaving for the airport, I gave my young roommates gifts of leftover coins for cab fare, OFF and aloe to deal with the bugs, apologies to the girls for my corny jokes and non-stop 90s references. For whatever reason I shouted "Boom-shock-a-lock-a" from the car as we drove away. I arrived back home on Saturday morning and just like that it was back to work on Monday.

Chapter 15

Thailand ...Why Not? (A Necessary Change)

On my first week back from Brazil, one of the products on my desk was an early prototype for a concept and soon product known as Cat Headphones. It was basically your typical headphones, but with cat ears on the headband which had external speakers to disperse your music to the masses. It was a tough product to wrap my head around in terms of need as I had just come back from weeks with kids that barely had food or clothing, let alone a need for cat ear shaped headphones.

I continued to wrestle with my Brazil experience for some time and struggled to find other ways to make an impact. You might say I left the experience, but the experience never left me. I thought about joining the Big Brothers / Big Sisters Program, but the one year commitment you had to make initially made me skittish and I decided not to pursue it. Holidays hit and I reached out to several shelters to offer help, but was turned away, because they already had enough volunteers. Fortunately, I was able to get involved with a few events helping at the local chapters of the Special Olympics, but still felt something was missing. I reached out to several alumni from the Cross Cultural Solutions Program that all lamented that the months following the experience were always tough.

As the months passed I tried to find other ways to find balance in my life outside of work. I took up hiking and really enjoyed the peace and nature that came from climbing the beautiful White Mountains of New Hampshire. There's something quite serene about being away from technology in the fresh air with the challenge of jumping from rock to rock until you make it to the top.

From hiking I tried the workouts of CrossFit, which were intense cardio and strength training that instantly brought me back to some of the college basketball workouts that used to leave me huddled in a fetal position after a workout had finished. It was fun, new and every workout was varied.

At this point, I also figured why not go back to school. I applied and was accepted to the University of Massachusetts Lowell Plastics Engineering Master's Program where the plan was to first obtain a Product Design certificate and complete 2 years of school work. The program was one of the top Plastics Engineering programs in the country and I was looking forward to going back to school again, but something still was missing. I had all of these things before me, but still was just going through the motions. I thought about other jobs and other locations, but figured I wasn't going to find a job that challenged me with different products like Brookstone. Other locations were interesting considerations (especially to escape from harsh northeastern winters), but figured I would end up in the same patterns I had before… school, work and sports with the same flatlined level of fulfillment.

I had made a friend in NH who had similar interests and also was in a point in her life where she needed a jolt. She mentioned the idea of quitting our jobs and going to Thailand for a year. I thought why not? On the surface, I suppose it sounded a bit crazy, but figured now was the time to again try something new and determine what truly made me happy. The new challenge was exciting and I was intrigued.

I withdrew from the 2nd Master's program I was accepted into and again prepared for the dreaded day of telling my work crew that I was leaving. My boss was very supportive and allowed me to individually tell everyone in the office that I was leaving. It was a tough day to say the least, but I was grateful for the one-on-one time to talk to the people I had worked so closely with for several years.

As work ended and the focus shifted to packing, selling and getting rid of everything I owned, I was faced with decisions like: Do I keep my old school gray box Nintendo (with Duck Hunt and Super Mario Brothers cartridges)? Do I throw out my green ninja turtle jacket? Should I donate my bongos I got from Australia a number of years ago? Tough decisions were before me, but one by one I got rid of everything I owned with the exception of one box of sentimental items that I could not part with. I must say, out of all the things I got rid of, the hardest thing to relinquish was not my car or clothes, but my books I had acquired over the years, tons and tons of books from school, travel and just entertaining reads. I donated these gems and got the bookstore to take several George Carlin masterpieces, the dozen sociology books I had read for my PhD fail years prior, textbooks galore and other fun reads from budding comedians to Frederick Douglas biographies and Charles Manson court trials. There was range.

With two bags containing everything that I owned, I hopped a plane with my friend and we headed to Chiang Mai, Thailand. Chiang Mai is an interesting place. It's filled with a huge expat community of temporary Americans, Australians, English, French and more living abroad among the locals. It's typically a pretty easy city to adjust to with all the modern conveniences you need like malls, plenty of delicious foods and is very easy to get around and more importantly it is ridiculously cheap. And by cheap, I mean $1 and $2 meals were commonplace. Sprinkle in cafes, Thai massage places, 7-11s and street meat on every corner and you have this city in northern Thailand. However, traveling has a way of testing your core. In many cases, you're thrown into situations on such an accelerated rate that things just seem more intense and more real when you're away from home. Thailand was no different for me and in a span of several months I had experienced five personal traumas (all involving loss of some sort) that forced me to re-evaluate what I was currently doing, what I wanted to do and who I wanted to surround myself with. Armed with these new questions, I headed south to the island of Koh Lanta.

Chapter 16

Moving to an Island ....Let's Start a Business (Koh Lanta and Portugal)

I never thought of myself as a Gilligan's Island gal, but the island of Koh Lanta (southern portion of Thailand) was a nice change of pace. I had made it to the island briefly a few weeks prior for New Years to spend the holiday with some friends. It was a grand time and I made some lifelong bonds with a few folks there. However, there was one conversation on the island that changed my life forever. I randomly bumped into a guy that I'd met in a basement floor eatery in Chiang Mai a month or so prior. Neither of us knew we would both be on the island, but we talked and met up for dinner later that night. We got on the subject of passions. Some people go with "you must be tired, you've been running around in my head all day", I typically approached the awkward guy/girl meet ups with "what are you passionate about?" (And tried to keep a straight face). I had played off this question when asked with answers like "bowling alleys" and "staring contests". No reaction from him. Instead he started sharing what he was passionate about which was being an actor in Japanese movies. I waited, not knowing if this was a joke or not. He was not Japanese (not that it matters I suppose), and it was the last thing I expected. He continued with surprising confidence about how everything he did was to work toward this goal and that it would happen, it was just a question of when, so why do anything different? Which got me thinking, what did I truly enjoy and what could I make a business out of? I knew I didn't want to be an Asian film star, but I did enjoy mentoring students from my days guest lecturing and working with interns at my previous companies. Dinner ended and a seed was again planted.

After a wonderful New Years, I flew back to Chiang Mai to finish out my apartment lease and grab my things (a few markers, some flip flops and 3 t-shirts). However, before leaving I attended a "Women's Entrepreneurs" Facebook Meetup with my good friend, Annelise. Not knowing what I would get out of this except free beverages and snacks, I actually left the meeting feeling even more inspired when the 2-hour event ended. I was surrounded by about 60 women, all different ages and ethnicities, and one by one, each person stood up, introduced herself and said what she was working on and needed help with. I was amazed as the women had all different projects that ranged from app development to software SEO stuff to natural healers. I stood up and, of course first apologized for the corny jokes that everyone was about to hear, then said I was working on an idea to help students figure out what to do after college and that I would be moving to an island to do this. I made so many connections that night and met so many wonderful people. I couldn't wait to get to work. A few weeks later I moved back to the island, Koh Lanta, and got to work on determining my target audience, what I would offer, what my website would look like and all of the stuff that goes into crafting a business. It was good to have a project again and one that I was (looks around nervously)......passionate about. I decided that under my LLC, I would call my business "What Do I Do After College", figuring why not just get to the point. I later expanded on this and crafted another business that would go hand-in-hand with the mentoring, but focus on engineering consulting (to help people craft their own product ideas into viable products on the market) and online education. It was a meaty mix.

I put in quite a bit of work on the island in between beech sunsets and scooter rides. Koh Lanta was wonderful, but I needed a change in scenery. Furthermore, my visa was about to run out, so I had no choice but to leave the country. I scoured the internet looking for someplace to land for at least a month and came across Lisbon, Portugal. The people apparently spoke English, so it would be easy for me to get around. There was a CrossFit gym, so I'd have something to keep me busy outside of work and it just looked cool.

I landed in Lisbon and found an apartment in the heart of the area, Bairre Alto, for a month's stay. How would I describe Lisbon? Well, she is a great temptress. She lures you in with pastel colored buildings, pastries and wine at every corner then makes you climb San Francisco-like cobble stoned hills as a punishment for taking part in the great city. Quite frankly, four weeks there and I was winded, but was loving the time in a completely different culture. It was a tad chilly (65-degree winter), but I used the time to write this book. Again, why not? I'd never written a book before. I wasn't famous, I wasn't planning on going on Oprah, and my sports career was not one to be analyzed and documented in novel form. Prior to this, my longest paper in school (outside of my Master's thesis that was littered with charts and pictures) was probably 16 pages…. double spaced …..with 1.5" margins …..and 13.5 font and I more than likely used the hated Comic Sans font type. So, Koh Lanta was starting a business and Lisbon was writing a book. My time was almost up in Lisbon when I needed to figure out where to go next. I had worked on an opportunity at a University in Thailand to teach in their Engineering Department, but a few red flags about the school and the poor air quality of northern Thailand at that point in the year steered me from going back to the land of the street meat. Lucky for me, a week prior I had come across an article about the island of Malta. At first I was initially drawn to Malta because I presumed it was named after a chocolatey drink, but soon Googled the location to find that it was an island somewhere between Northern Africa and Sicily. It sounded perfect. So, I packed up my things: markers, flip flops, 3 t-shirts and a bag full of pastries that I would try and smuggle into the next country.

Chapter 17

Malta, Malta, Malta ...the End, but not Really

I landed in Malta and was instantly taken aback by the beauty of the island. One of the first things I noticed was the plethora of Italian eateries (one actually named "Margo"). I had gone from Portugal pastries to perfect pizza in Malta. By golly, this was going to be good. Aside from the nuances of the city that were all exciting, I was still crafting a business and with anything new, there's a lot to get used to and learn.

Starting a business is not all sunshine and rainbows, especially when you are overseas and have taken a chance with only a backpack, the meagre remains of a bank account, and the belief that you will be successful. It's a challenge. Surprisingly, one thing that's kept me going throughout this process is the message in the Katy Perry

Olympics song, Rise. I randomly put it on the other day and was struck by the lyrics of the song, "I won't just survive, oh you will see me thrive". I've probably listened to this song 100 times since I recently happened across it, but the message is simple and it carries a punch. Translation: perseverance, belief and urgency are key.

Well, this is the end of the book, but it certainly isn't the end of the journey. If there's one thing I've learned is there's more than one way to go through life. With all the ridiculousness in my personal journey--the trips, the schools and even the zip lines--the one thing that's been consistent is the notion to simply TRY. Try to go outside your comfort zone, try to do something that others think is ridiculous or may not understand, try to help someone else and try to get one of those jokes to land. It's been over 30 years and I'm still working on that last one :). As I continue to build my business, continue to work with students, maybe even take another stab at a PhD or marathon, and continue to travel to far off places (by the time you're reading this I've probably moved to another country/continent), I urge you to continue your journey and craft what fulfills you. If you build it, Life will come.

Peace in the Middle East (and all over the World). Thank you for reading this and a few other thank yous to some special characters in my life:

- *My Parents* aka the creators for their support
- *My Sister* aka Giggles for always looking out for me
- *BCK* for taking a chance on a girl wearing rec specs and saying "hello"
- *Dub* for co-writing the Sasquash Times
- *Serg* for surviving college basketball together (among other things)
- *Val* for being an inspiration with your continued fight and also being freaking hilarious

- *Sarah* for being at a level of cool that I will never achieve and for your folks for coaching me up

- *Kim* for listening and steering me in the right direction

- *Annelise* for being a true friend and my accountability partner

- *Mike* for believing in me and my business and more importantly being a Seinfeld and Jim Carrey fan

Thanks for reading. I would love to hear from you!

info@MargotSandy.com

Made in the USA
Columbia, SC
22 February 2018